# Wedding Planner ♡

# Wedding Planner...

♡

**WEDDING DATE & TIME:**

**VENUE ADDRESS:**

**BUDGET:**

**OFFICIANT:**

**WEDDING PARTY:**

**NOTES & REMINDERS:**

**TO DO LIST:**

# Wedding Budget...

| | TOTAL COST: | DEPOSIT: | REMAINDER: |
|---|---|---|---|
| WEDDING VENUE | | | |
| RECEPTION VENUE | | | |
| FLORIST | | | |
| OFFICIANT | | | |
| CATERER | | | |
| WEDDING CAKE | | | |
| BRIDAL ATTIRE | | | |
| BRIDAL ATTIRE | | | |
| BRIDAL JEWELRY | | | |
| BRIDESMAIDS ATTIRE | | | |
| BRIDESMEN ATTIRE | | | |
| HAIR & MAKE UP | | | |
| PHOTOGRAPHER | | | |
| VIDEOGRAPHER | | | |
| DJ SERVICE/ENTERTAINMENT | | | |
| INVITATIONS | | | |
| TRANSPORTATION | | | |
| WEDDING PARTY GIFTS | | | |
| RENTALS | | | |
| HONEYMOON | | | |

# 12 Months Before...

SET THE DATE

SET YOUR BUDGET

CHOOSE YOUR THEME

ORGANIZE ENGAGEMENT PARTY

RESEARCH VENUES

BOOK A WEDDING PLANNER

RESEARCH PHOTOGRAPHERS

RESEARCH VIDEOGRAPHERS

RESEARCH DJ'S/ENTERTAINMENT

CONSIDER FLORISTS

RESEARCH CATERERS

DECIDE ON OFFICIANT

CREATE INITIAL GUEST LIST

CHOOSE WEDDING PARTY

SHOP FOR WEDDING DRESSES

REGISTER WITH GIFT REGISTRY

DISCUSS HONEYMOON IDEAS

RESEARCH WEDDING RINGS

THINGS TO REMEMBER:

# 9 Months Before...

FINALIZE GUEST LIST

CHOOSE WEDDING GOWNS

ORDER INVITATIONS

ORDER BRIDESMAIDS DRESSES

PLAN YOUR RECEPTION

RESERVE TUXEDOS

BOOK PHOTOGRAPHER

ARRANGE TRANSPORTATION

BOOK VIDEOGRAPHER

BOOK WEDDING VENUE

BOOK FLORIST

BOOK RECEPTION VENUE

BOOK DJ/ENTERTAINMENT

PLAN HONEYMOON

BOOK CATERER

BOOK OFFICIANT

CHOOSE WEDDING CAKE

BOOK ROOMS FOR GUESTS

THINGS TO REMEMBER:

# 6 Months Before...

ORDER THANK YOU NOTES

REVIEW RECEPTION DETAILS

MAKE APPT FOR DRESS FITTINGS

CONFIRM BRIDESMAIDS DRESSES

GET MARRIAGE LICENSE

BOOK HAIR/MAKE UP STYLIST

CONFIRM MUSIC SELECTIONS

PLAN BRIDAL SHOWER

PLAN REHEARSAL

SHOP FOR WEDDING RINGS

THINGS TO REMEMBER:

# 3 Months Before...

MAIL OUT INVITATIONS

MEET WITH OFFICIANT

BUY GIFTS FOR WEDDING PARTY

BOOK FINAL GOWN FITTINGS

BUY WEDDING BANDS

PLAN YOUR HAIR STYLE

PURCHASE SHOES/HEELS

CONFIRM PASSPORTS ARE VALID

FINALIZE RECEPTION MENU

PLAN REHEARSAL DINNER

CONFIRM ALL BOOKINGS

APPLY FOR MARRIAGE LICENSE

CONFIRM MUSIC SELECTIONS

DRAFT WEDDING VOWS

CHOOSE YOUR MC

ARRANGE AIRPORT TRANSFER

THINGS TO REMEMBER:

# 1 Month Before...

CONFIRM FINAL GUEST COUNT

CONFIRM RECEPTION DETAILS

ATTEND FINAL GOWN FITTINGS

CONFIRM PHOTOGRAPHER

WRAP WEDDING PARTY GIFTS

CREATE PHOTOGRAPHY SHOT LIST

REHEARSE WEDDING VOWS

BOOK MANI-PEDI

CONFIRM WITH FLORIST

CONFIRM VIDEOGRAPHER

PICK UP BRIDESMAIDS DRESSES

CREATE WEDDING SCHEDULE

 THINGS TO REMEMBER:

# 1 Week Before...

| | |
|---|---|
| FINALIZE SEATING PLANS | DELIVER LICENSE TO OFFICIANT |
| MAKE PAYMENTS TO VENDORS | CONFIRM WITH BAKERY |
| PACK FOR HONEYMOON | PICK UP WEDDING DRESSES |
| CONFIRM HOTEL RESERVATIONS | PICK UP TUXEDOS |
| GIVE SCHEDULE TO PARTY | GIVE MUSIC LIST TO DJ |

THINGS TO REMEMBER:

# 1 Week Before...

| | THINGS TO DO: | NOTES: |
|---|---|---|
| **MONDAY** | | |
| **TUESDAY** | | |
| **WEDNESDAY** | | |
| **THURSDAY** | | |

REMINDERS & NOTES:

# 1 Week Before...

|  | THINGS TO DO: | NOTES: |
|---|---|---|
| **FRIDAY** | | |
| **SATURDAY** | | |
| **SUNDAY** | | |

LEFT TO DO:

REMINDERS:                                    NOTES:

# The Day Before...

GET MANICURE/PEDICURE

ATTEND REHEARSAL DINNER

GET A GOOD NIGHT'S SLEEP!

GIVE GIFTS TO WEDDING PARTY

FINALIZE PACKING

TO DO LIST:

# The Big Day!

GET HAIR & MAKE UP DONE

HAVE A HEALTHY BREAKFAST

ENJOY YOUR BIG DAY!

MEET WITH BRIDESMAIDS/MEN

GIVE RINGS TO BEST MAN/WOMAN

TO DO LIST:

# Wedding Planner...

**ENGAGEMENT PARTY:**

DATE:                              LOCATION:

TIME:                              NUMBER OF GUESTS:

NOTES:

**BRIDAL SHOWER:**

DATE:                              LOCATION:

TIME:                              NUMBER OF GUESTS:

NOTES:

**DOE & DOE/HEN&HEN PARTY:**

DATE:                              LOCATION:

TIME:                              NUMBER OF GUESTS:

NOTES:

# Wedding Party

**BRIDE 1:**

**MAID/MATRON OF HONOR:**

PHONE:                DRESS SIZE:              SHOE SIZE:

EMAIL:

**BRIDESMAID:**

PHONE:                DRESS SIZE:              SHOE SIZE:

EMAIL:

**BRIDESMAID #2:**

PHONE:                DRESS SIZE:              SHOE SIZE:

EMAIL:

**BRIDESMAID #3:**

PHONE:                DRESS SIZE:              SHOE SIZE:

EMAIL:

**BRIDESMAID #4:**

PHONE:                DRESS SIZE:              SHOE SIZE:

EMAIL:

# Wedding Party

**BRIDE 2**
**MAID/MATRON OF HONOR:**

PHONE:                    DRESS SIZE:                    SHOE SIZE:

EMAIL:

**BRIDESMAID:**

PHONE:                    DRESS SIZE:                    SHOE SIZE:

EMAIL:

**BRIDESMAID #2:**

PHONE:                    DRESS SIZE:                    SHOE SIZE:

EMAIL:

**BRIDESMAID #3:**

PHONE:                    DRESS SIZE:                    SHOE SIZE:

EMAIL:

**BRIDESMAID #4:**

PHONE:                    DRESS SIZE:                    SHOE SIZE:

EMAIL:

# Wedding Party

**OTHER OPTIONS:**

**BEST MAN:**

PHONE:                          WAIST SIZE:                          SHOE SIZE:

NECK SIZE:                      SLEEVE SIZE:                         JACKET SIZE:

EMAIL:


**BRIDESMAN #1:**

PHONE:                          WAIST SIZE:                          SHOE SIZE:

NECK SIZE:                      SLEEVE SIZE:                         JACKET SIZE:

EMAIL:


**BRIDESMAN #2:**

PHONE:                          WAIST SIZE:                          SHOE SIZE:

NECK SIZE:                      SLEEVE SIZE:                         JACKET SIZE:

EMAIL:


**BRIDESMAN #3:**

PHONE:                          WAIST SIZE:                          SHOE SIZE:

NECK SIZE:                      SLEEVE SIZE:                         JACKET SIZE:

EMAIL:


**BRIDESMAN #4:**

PHONE:                          WAIST SIZE:                          SHOE SIZE:

NECK SIZE:                      SLEEVE SIZE:                         JACKET SIZE:

EMAIL:

# Photographer

**PHOTOGRAPHER:**

PHONE:                          COMPANY:

EMAIL:                          ADDRESS:

**WEDDING PACKAGE OVERVIEW:**

EST PRICE:

| **INCLUSIONS:** | YES ✓ | NO ✓ | COST: |
|---|---|---|---|
| ENGAGEMENT SHOOT: | | | |
| PHOTO ALBUMNS: | | | |
| FRAMES: | | | |
| PROOFS INCLUDED: | | | |
| NEGATIVES INCLUDED: | | | |

**TOTAL COST:**

# Videographer

**VIDEOGRAPHER:**

PHONE:                          COMPANY:

EMAIL:                          ADDRESS:

**WEDDING PACKAGE OVERVIEW:**

EST PRICE:

**INCLUSIONS:**          YES  ✓      NO  ✓      COST:

DUPLICATES/COPIES:

PHOTO MONTAGE:

MUSIC ADDED:

EDITING:

**TOTAL COST:**

# DJ/Entertainment

**DJ/LIVE BAND/ENTERTAINMENT:**

PHONE:                          COMPANY:

EMAIL:                          ADDRESS:

START TIME:                     END TIME:

**ENTERTAINMENT SERVICE OVERVIEW:**

EST PRICE:

| **INCLUSIONS:** | YES ✓ | NO ✓ | COST: |
|---|---|---|---|
| SOUND EQUIPMENT: | | | |
| LIGHTING: | | | |
| SPECIAL EFFECTS: | | | |
| GRATUITIES | | | |

**TOTAL COST:**

# Florist Planner

**FLORIST:**

PHONE:                          COMPANY:

EMAIL:                          ADDRESS:

**FLORAL PACKAGE:**

EST PRICE: _____

**INCLUSIONS:**        YES  ✓      NO  ✓      COST:

BRIDAL BOUQUET:

THROW AWAY BOUQUET:

CORSAGES:

CEREMONY FLOWERS

CENTERPIECES

CAKE TOPPER

BOUTONNIERE

**TOTAL COST:**

# Wedding Cake

PHONE:                 COMPANY:

EMAIL:                  ADDRESS:

**WEDDING CAKE PACKAGE:**

♡

COST: _____ FREE TASTING: _____ DELIVERY FEE: _____

FLAVOR:

FILLING:

SIZE:

SHAPE:

COLOR:

EXTRAS:

**TOTAL COST:**

# Transportation Planner

**TO CEREMONY:**          PICK UP TIME:          PICK UP LOCATION:

BRIDE 1:

BRIDE 2:

BRIDE'S PARENTS:

BRIDES'S PARENTS:

BRIDESMAIDS:

BRIDESMEN:

**NOTES:**

**TO RECEPTION:**          PICK UP TIME:          PICK UP LOCATION:

BRIDE & BRIDE:

BRIDE'S PARENTS:

BRIDES'S PARENTS:

BRIDESMAIDS:

BRIDESMEN:

# *Wedding Planner...*

**BACHELORETTE PARTY:**

DATE:                          LOCATION:

TIME:                          NUMBER OF GUESTS:

 NOTES:


**BACHELORETTE PARTY:**

DATE:                          LOCATION:

TIME:                          NUMBER OF GUESTS:

 NOTES:


**CEREMONY REHEARSAL:**

DATE:                          LOCATION:

TIME:                          NUMBER OF GUESTS:

 NOTES:

# Wedding Planner...

**REHEARSAL DINNER:**

DATE:                                    LOCATION:

TIME:                                    NUMBER OF GUESTS:

NOTES:

**RECEPTION:**

DATE:                                    LOCATION:

TIME:                                    NUMBER OF GUESTS:

NOTES:

REMINDERS:

# Names & Addresses

**CEREMONY:**

PHONE: _____          CONTACT NAME: _____

EMAIL: _____          ADDRESS: _____

**RECEPTION:**

PHONE: _____          CONTACT NAME: _____

EMAIL: _____          ADDRESS: _____

**OFFICIANT:**

PHONE: _____          CONTACT NAME: _____

EMAIL: _____          ADDRESS: _____

**WEDDING PLANNER:**

PHONE: _____          CONTACT NAME: _____

EMAIL: _____          ADDRESS: _____

# Names & Addresses

**CATERER:**

PHONE:

CONTACT NAME:

EMAIL:

ADDRESS:

**FLORIST:**

PHONE:

CONTACT NAME:

EMAIL:

ADDRESS:

**BAKERY:**

PHONE:

CONTACT NAME:

EMAIL:

ADDRESS:

**BRIDAL SHOP:**

PHONE:

CONTACT NAME:

EMAIL:

ADDRESS:

# Names & Addresses

**PHOTOGRAPHER:**

PHONE:                          CONTACT NAME:

EMAIL:                          ADDRESS:

**VIDEOGRAPHER:**

PHONE:                          CONTACT NAME:

EMAIL:                          ADDRESS:

**DJ/ENTERTAINMENT:**

PHONE:                          CONTACT NAME:

EMAIL:                          ADDRESS:

**HAIR/NAIL SALON:**

PHONE:                          CONTACT NAME:

EMAIL:                          ADDRESS:

# Names & Addresses

**MAKE UP ARTIST:**

PHONE:                          CONTACT NAME:

EMAIL:                          ADDRESS:

**RENTALS:**

PHONE:                          CONTACT NAME:

EMAIL:                          ADDRESS:

**HONEYMOON RESORT/HOTEL:**

PHONE:                          CONTACT NAME:

EMAIL:                          ADDRESS:

**TRANSPORTATION SERVICE:**

PHONE:                          CONTACT NAME:

EMAIL:                          ADDRESS:

# Caterer Details

**CONTACT INFORMATION:**

PHONE:                         CONTACT NAME:

EMAIL:                         ADDRESS:

**MENU CHOICE #1:**

**MENU CHOICE #2:**

|  | YES ✓ | NO ✓ | COST: |
|---|---|---|---|
| BAR INCLUDED: | | | |
| CORKAGE FEE: | | | |
| HORS D'OEURS: | | | |
| TAXES INCLUDED: | | | |
| GRATUITIES INCLUDED: | | | |

# Menu Planner

**HORS D'OEUVRES**

**1st COURSE:**

**2nd COURSE:**

**3rd COURSE:**

**4th COURSE:**

**DESSERT:**

# Menu Planner

**COFFEE/TEA:**

**FRUIT:**

**SWEETS TABLE:**

**WEDDING CAKE:**

**NOTES:**

# Wedding Guest List

| NAME: | ADDRESS: | # IN PARTY: | RSVP✓ |
|---|---|---|---|
| | | | |
| | | | |
| | | | |
| | | | |
| | | | |
| | | | |
| | | | |
| | | | |
| | | | |
| | | | |
| | | | |
| | | | |
| | | | |
| | | | |
| | | | |
| | | | |
| | | | |
| | | | |
| | | | |
| | | | |

# Wedding Guest List

| NAME: | ADDRESS: | # IN PARTY: | RSVP✓ |
|---|---|---|---|
|  |  |  |  |
|  |  |  |  |
|  |  |  |  |
|  |  |  |  |
|  |  |  |  |
|  |  |  |  |
|  |  |  |  |
|  |  |  |  |
|  |  |  |  |
|  |  |  |  |
|  |  |  |  |
|  |  |  |  |
|  |  |  |  |
|  |  |  |  |
|  |  |  |  |
|  |  |  |  |
|  |  |  |  |
|  |  |  |  |
|  |  |  |  |

# Wedding Guest List

| NAME: | ADDRESS: | # IN PARTY: | RSVP✓ |
|-------|----------|-------------|-------|
|       |          |             |       |
|       |          |             |       |
|       |          |             |       |
|       |          |             |       |
|       |          |             |       |
|       |          |             |       |
|       |          |             |       |
|       |          |             |       |
|       |          |             |       |
|       |          |             |       |
|       |          |             |       |
|       |          |             |       |
|       |          |             |       |
|       |          |             |       |
|       |          |             |       |
|       |          |             |       |
|       |          |             |       |
|       |          |             |       |
|       |          |             |       |

# Wedding Guest List

| NAME: | ADDRESS: | # IN PARTY: | RSVP✓ |
|-------|----------|-------------|-------|
|       |          |             |       |
|       |          |             |       |
|       |          |             |       |
|       |          |             |       |
|       |          |             |       |
|       |          |             |       |
|       |          |             |       |
|       |          |             |       |
|       |          |             |       |
|       |          |             |       |
|       |          |             |       |
|       |          |             |       |
|       |          |             |       |
|       |          |             |       |
|       |          |             |       |
|       |          |             |       |
|       |          |             |       |
|       |          |             |       |

# Wedding Guest List

| NAME: | ADDRESS: | # IN PARTY: | RSVP✓ |
|---|---|---|---|
|  |  |  |  |
|  |  |  |  |
|  |  |  |  |
|  |  |  |  |
|  |  |  |  |
|  |  |  |  |
|  |  |  |  |
|  |  |  |  |
|  |  |  |  |
|  |  |  |  |
|  |  |  |  |
|  |  |  |  |
|  |  |  |  |
|  |  |  |  |
|  |  |  |  |
|  |  |  |  |
|  |  |  |  |
|  |  |  |  |

# Wedding Guest List

| NAME: | ADDRESS: | # IN PARTY: | RSVP✓ |
|-------|----------|-------------|-------|
|       |          |             |       |
|       |          |             |       |
|       |          |             |       |
|       |          |             |       |
|       |          |             |       |
|       |          |             |       |
|       |          |             |       |
|       |          |             |       |
|       |          |             |       |
|       |          |             |       |
|       |          |             |       |
|       |          |             |       |
|       |          |             |       |
|       |          |             |       |
|       |          |             |       |
|       |          |             |       |
|       |          |             |       |
|       |          |             |       |
|       |          |             |       |

# Wedding Guest List

| NAME: | ADDRESS: | # IN PARTY: | RSVP✓ |
|---|---|---|---|
| | | | |
| | | | |
| | | | |
| | | | |
| | | | |
| | | | |
| | | | |
| | | | |
| | | | |
| | | | |
| | | | |
| | | | |
| | | | |
| | | | |
| | | | |
| | | | |
| | | | |
| | | | |
| | | | |

# Wedding Guest List

| NAME: | ADDRESS: | # IN PARTY: | RSVP✓ |
|-------|----------|-------------|-------|
|  |  |  |  |
|  |  |  |  |
|  |  |  |  |
|  |  |  |  |
|  |  |  |  |
|  |  |  |  |
|  |  |  |  |
|  |  |  |  |
|  |  |  |  |
|  |  |  |  |
|  |  |  |  |
|  |  |  |  |
|  |  |  |  |
|  |  |  |  |
|  |  |  |  |
|  |  |  |  |
|  |  |  |  |
|  |  |  |  |
|  |  |  |  |
|  |  |  |  |

# Wedding Guest List

| NAME: | ADDRESS: | # IN PARTY: | RSVP✓ |
|---|---|---|---|
| | | | |
| | | | |
| | | | |
| | | | |
| | | | |
| | | | |
| | | | |
| | | | |
| | | | |
| | | | |
| | | | |
| | | | |
| | | | |
| | | | |
| | | | |
| | | | |
| | | | |
| | | | |

# Wedding Guest List

| NAME: | ADDRESS: | # IN PARTY: | RSVP√ |
|-------|----------|-------------|-------|
|  |  |  |  |
|  |  |  |  |
|  |  |  |  |
|  |  |  |  |
|  |  |  |  |
|  |  |  |  |
|  |  |  |  |
|  |  |  |  |
|  |  |  |  |
|  |  |  |  |
|  |  |  |  |
|  |  |  |  |
|  |  |  |  |
|  |  |  |  |
|  |  |  |  |
|  |  |  |  |
|  |  |  |  |
|  |  |  |  |
|  |  |  |  |
|  |  |  |  |

# Wedding Guest List

| NAME: | ADDRESS: | # IN PARTY: | RSVP✓ |
|---|---|---|---|
| | | | |
| | | | |
| | | | |
| | | | |
| | | | |
| | | | |
| | | | |
| | | | |
| | | | |
| | | | |
| | | | |
| | | | |
| | | | |
| | | | |
| | | | |
| | | | |
| | | | |
| | | | |
| | | | |

# Wedding Guest List

| NAME: | ADDRESS: | # IN PARTY: | RSVP✓ |
|---|---|---|---|
| | | | |
| | | | |
| | | | |
| | | | |
| | | | |
| | | | |
| | | | |
| | | | |
| | | | |
| | | | |
| | | | |
| | | | |
| | | | |
| | | | |
| | | | |
| | | | |
| | | | |
| | | | |
| | | | |

# Wedding Guest List

| NAME: | ADDRESS: | # IN PARTY: | RSVP✓ |
|---|---|---|---|
|  |  |  |  |
|  |  |  |  |
|  |  |  |  |
|  |  |  |  |
|  |  |  |  |
|  |  |  |  |
|  |  |  |  |
|  |  |  |  |
|  |  |  |  |
|  |  |  |  |
|  |  |  |  |
|  |  |  |  |
|  |  |  |  |
|  |  |  |  |
|  |  |  |  |
|  |  |  |  |
|  |  |  |  |
|  |  |  |  |
|  |  |  |  |

# Wedding Guest List

| NAME: | ADDRESS: | # IN PARTY: | RSVP✓ |
|---|---|---|---|
|  |  |  |  |
|  |  |  |  |
|  |  |  |  |
|  |  |  |  |
|  |  |  |  |
|  |  |  |  |
|  |  |  |  |
|  |  |  |  |
|  |  |  |  |
|  |  |  |  |
|  |  |  |  |
|  |  |  |  |
|  |  |  |  |
|  |  |  |  |
|  |  |  |  |
|  |  |  |  |
|  |  |  |  |
|  |  |  |  |
|  |  |  |  |

# Wedding Guest List

| NAME: | ADDRESS: | # IN PARTY: | RSVP✓ |
|---|---|---|---|
| | | | |
| | | | |
| | | | |
| | | | |
| | | | |
| | | | |
| | | | |
| | | | |
| | | | |
| | | | |
| | | | |
| | | | |
| | | | |
| | | | |
| | | | |
| | | | |
| | | | |
| | | | |
| | | | |

# Wedding Guest List

| NAME: | ADDRESS: | # IN PARTY: | RSVP✓ |
|---|---|---|---|
| | | | |
| | | | |
| | | | |
| | | | |
| | | | |
| | | | |
| | | | |
| | | | |
| | | | |
| | | | |
| | | | |
| | | | |
| | | | |
| | | | |
| | | | |
| | | | |
| | | | |
| | | | |
| | | | |

# Wedding Guest List

| NAME: | ADDRESS: | # IN PARTY: | RSVP✓ |
|---|---|---|---|
| | | | |
| | | | |
| | | | |
| | | | |
| | | | |
| | | | |
| | | | |
| | | | |
| | | | |
| | | | |
| | | | |
| | | | |
| | | | |
| | | | |
| | | | |
| | | | |
| | | | |
| | | | |
| | | | |

# Wedding Guest List

| NAME: | ADDRESS: | # IN PARTY: | RSVP✓ |
|---|---|---|---|
| | | | |
| | | | |
| | | | |
| | | | |
| | | | |
| | | | |
| | | | |
| | | | |
| | | | |
| | | | |
| | | | |
| | | | |
| | | | |
| | | | |
| | | | |
| | | | |
| | | | |
| | | | |
| | | | |

# Wedding Guest List

| NAME: | ADDRESS: | # IN PARTY: | RSVP✓ |
|-------|----------|-------------|-------|
|       |          |             |       |
|       |          |             |       |
|       |          |             |       |
|       |          |             |       |
|       |          |             |       |
|       |          |             |       |
|       |          |             |       |
|       |          |             |       |
|       |          |             |       |
|       |          |             |       |
|       |          |             |       |
|       |          |             |       |
|       |          |             |       |
|       |          |             |       |
|       |          |             |       |
|       |          |             |       |
|       |          |             |       |
|       |          |             |       |
|       |          |             |       |

# Wedding Guest List

| NAME: | ADDRESS: | # IN PARTY: | RSVP✓ |
|---|---|---|---|
| | | | |
| | | | |
| | | | |
| | | | |
| | | | |
| | | | |
| | | | |
| | | | |
| | | | |
| | | | |
| | | | |
| | | | |
| | | | |
| | | | |
| | | | |
| | | | |
| | | | |
| | | | |
| | | | |
| | | | |

# Seating Planner

Table #

Table #

# Seating Planner

Table #

Table #

# Seating Planner

Table #

Table #

# Seating Planner

Table #

Table #

# Seating Planner

Table #

Table #

# Seating Planner

Table #

Table #

# Seating Planner

## Table #

## Table #

# Seating Planner

Table #

Table #

# Seating Planner

Table #

Table #

# Seating Planner

Table #

Table #

# Seating Planner

Table #

Table #

# Seating Planner

Table #

Table #

# Seating Planner

Table #

Table #

# Seating Planner

Table #

Table #

# Seating Planner

Table #

Table #

# Seating Planner

Table #

Table #

# Seating Planner

Table #

Table #

# Seating Planner

Table #

Table #

# Seating Planner

Table #

Table #

# Seating Planner

Table #

Table #

# Seating Planner

Table #

Table #

# Seating Planner

Table #

Table #

# Seating Planner

Table #

Table #

# Seating Planner

Table #

Table #

# Seating Planner

Table #

Table #

# Seating Planner

Table #

Table #

Made in the USA
Las Vegas, NV
12 January 2022